First Facts® Map Mania

Up North and Down South

Using Map Directions

by Doreen Gonzales

Consultant: Susanna A. McMaster, PhD
Associate Director, MGIS Program
Geography Department, University of Minnesota

Hi everyone! I'm Ace McCaw. Do you ever get lost? Come on, I'll get you going in the right direction.

Capstone press®

Mankato, Minnesota

First Facts is published by Capstone Press,
151 Good Counsel Drive, P.O. Box 669, Mankato, Minnesota 56002.
www.capstonepress.com

Library of Congress Cataloging-in-Publication Data
Gonzales, Doreen.
    Up north and down south : using map directions / by Doreen Gonzales.
    p. cm. —(First facts. Map mania)
    Summary: "Describes the cardinal directions, north, south, east, and west, and how directions
are used with a map and compass"—Provided by publisher.
    Includes bibliographical references and index.
    ISBN-13: 978-1-4296-0055-2 (hardcover)
    ISBN-10: 1-4296-0055-1 (hardcover)
    ISBN-13: 978-1-4296-2881-5 (softcover pbk.)
    ISBN-10: 1-4296-2881-2 (softcover pbk.)
    1. Cardinal points—Juvenile literature. I. Title.
G108.5.C3G66 2008
912.01'4—dc22   2006100036

Editorial Credits
Jennifer Besel, editor; Bobbi J. Wyss, Veronica Bianchini, and Linda Clavel, designers; Bob Lentz,
    illustrator; Wanda Winch, photo researcher; Renee Doyle, map designer

Photo and Map Credits
Capstone Press/Karon Dubke, cover, 10 (both), 15, 17 (compass), 19 (compasses), 21
Folio Inc/Wally McNamee, 16
Maps.com, 4–5, 6–7, 9, 17 (maps)
MarksPhotographs.com/Mark G. Cappitella, 8
Shutterstock/Hiroyuki Saita, 20
Washington State Department of Ecology/Vantage Point Photography, 4 (photo)

1 2 3 4 5 6 12 11 10 09 08 07

Table of Contents

Help! How to Get Unlost 4

Beyond Left and Right 6

When Isn't a Rose a Flower? Only on a Map! 8

Point Me North: Compass Basics 10

Steps in the Right Direction 12

Practice Makes Perfect 16

Amazing but True!.. 20

Hands On: Make a Compass 21

Glossary.. 22

Read More 23

Internet Sites... 23

Index.. 24

Help! How to Get Unlost

Oh, no! You're lost and don't know which way to go. Map to the rescue! A map shows you what the world looks like from above. A map can easily tell you which way to fly (or walk, for those of you without wings).

President Point

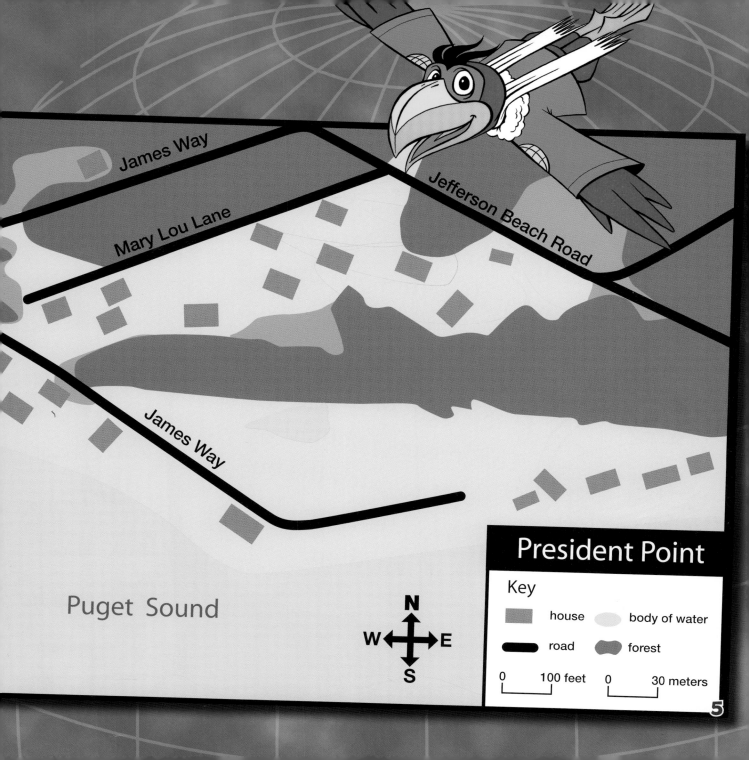

James Way

Mary Lou Lane

Jefferson Beach Road

James Way

Puget Sound

N
W E
S

President Point

Key

house

road

body of water

forest

0   100 feet   0   30 meters

Beyond Left and Right

So how do maps help us find our way? Maps show what **direction** one thing is from another. On the map, you can see the bus stop is to the right of my school. That means I should go east to catch the bus. Wonder how I knew that? Read on.

Key

school

bus stop

store

birdhouse

birdbath

direction—the way you're moving or pointing

6

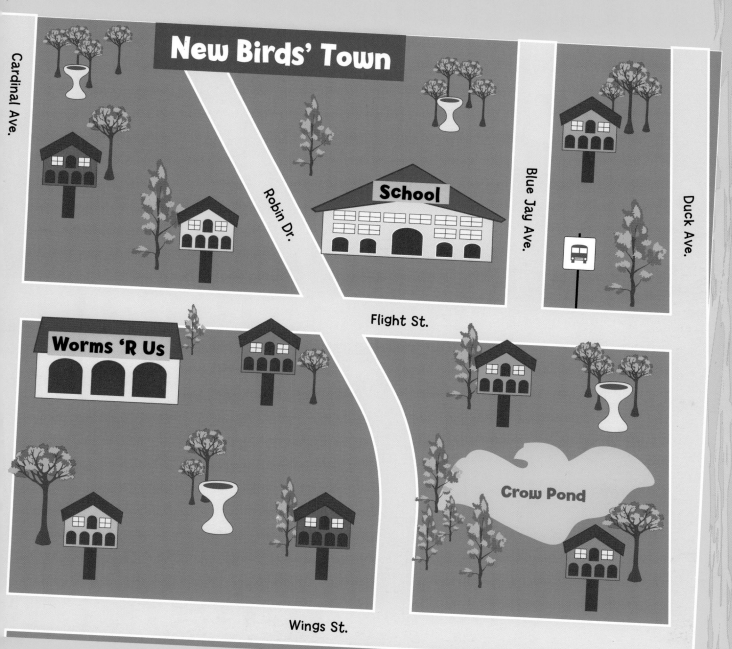

New Birds' Town

Cardinal Ave.

Robin Dr.

School

Blue Jay Ave.

Duck Ave.

Flight St.

Worms 'R Us

Crow Pond

Wings St.

Keep north at the top and you'll never look at a map upside down again.

Centerbook, CT

When Isn't a Rose a Flower? Only on a Map!

Maps have a label called a **compass rose**. The compass rose shows you which way is north, south, east, or west. Use the compass rose to tell which direction to go.

compass rose—the label on a map that shows the directions

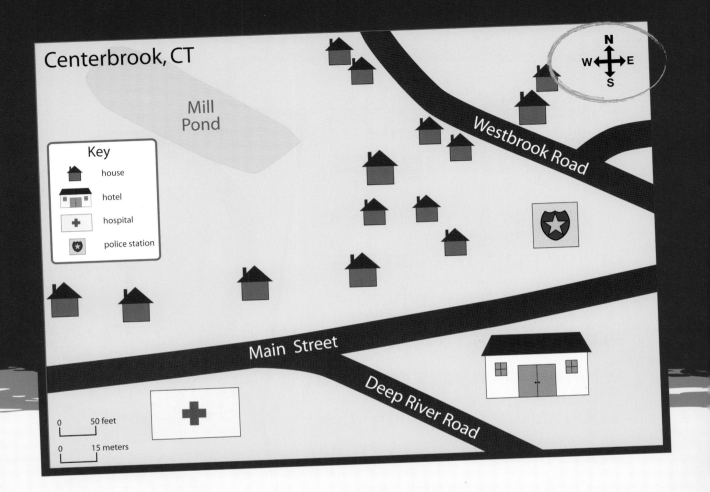

On the map, the hospital is left of the hotel. Which direction should I fly to get from the hotel to the hospital? Did you say west? I knew you were smart!

Point Me North: Compass Basics

Now you can find north on the map. But can you find north from where you're sitting? Here's where a **compass** comes in. The needle on a compass always points north. Twist the compass **dial** until the letter N is under the point of the needle. Now you're ready to go.

Needle

Compass dial

compass—a tool you can use to find what direction you are going

Try It!

You can use the sun to find north too. Go outside on a sunny morning before 9 o'clock. Stand so that you are facing the rising sun. Stretch out your arms and bingo! Your left hand is pointing north. This isn't the most accurate way to find north, but it will get you close.

Steps in the Right Direction

Using a map and compass together can be a little tricky at first. Follow these steps and you'll do just fine.

Step 1:
Hold your compass flat out in front of you. When the needle stops spinning, it will be pointing north.

Step 2: Turn the compass dial so the N lines up with the needle's point.

Step 3: Now turn yourself and your map so you are facing north.

Step 4: On the map, make sure north is on the top. Then find where you are and which direction you need to go.

14

Step 5: Use the compass to find that direction and get going.

Try It!

In orienteering, kids use a compass, a map, and a set of clues to race to a goal. You could set up a course in your school's playground. Write clues that tell players which direction to go. Hide the clues all around the playground. See if your friends can use a map of your school, a compass, and your clues to find their way to treats you have hidden!

15

Practice Makes Perfect

Let's pretend we're in Washington, D.C. We're standing at the Washington Monument. We need to go to the Capitol building. What do we do?

First, use your compass to find north where you're standing. Then, look at the map. Which direction is the Capitol? If you said east, you're right! Now find east on your compass and walk (or fly) that way.

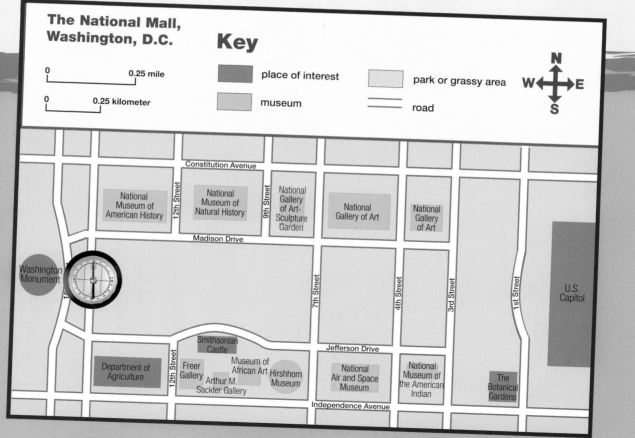

The National Mall, Washington, D.C.

Key

0 — 0.25 mile

0 — 0.25 kilometer

■ place of interest
■ museum
■ park or grassy area
═ road

N W E S

Constitution Avenue

National Museum of American History

12th Street

National Museum of Natural History

9th Street

National Gallery of Art-Sculpture Garden

National Gallery of Art

National Gallery of Art

Madison Drive

Washington Monument

7th Street

4th Street

3rd Street

1st Street

U.S. Capitol

Smithsonian Castle

Department of Agriculture

12th Street

Freer Gallery

Museum of African Art

Arthur M. Sackler Gallery

Hirshhorn Museum

Jefferson Drive

National Air and Space Museum

National Museum of the American Indian

The Botanical Gardens

Independence Avenue

Now we're at the zoo! You have to make some turns to get to the lions. No problem. Just stop before each turn. Line up your map and compass with north. Find the direction you need to go on the map and get moving. Using a compass and map will help you get to the lions. And you'll never end up in the monkey cage!

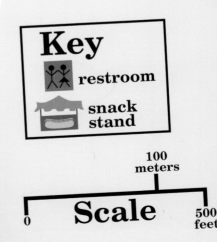

Key

restroom

snack stand

100 meters

Scale

0

500 feet

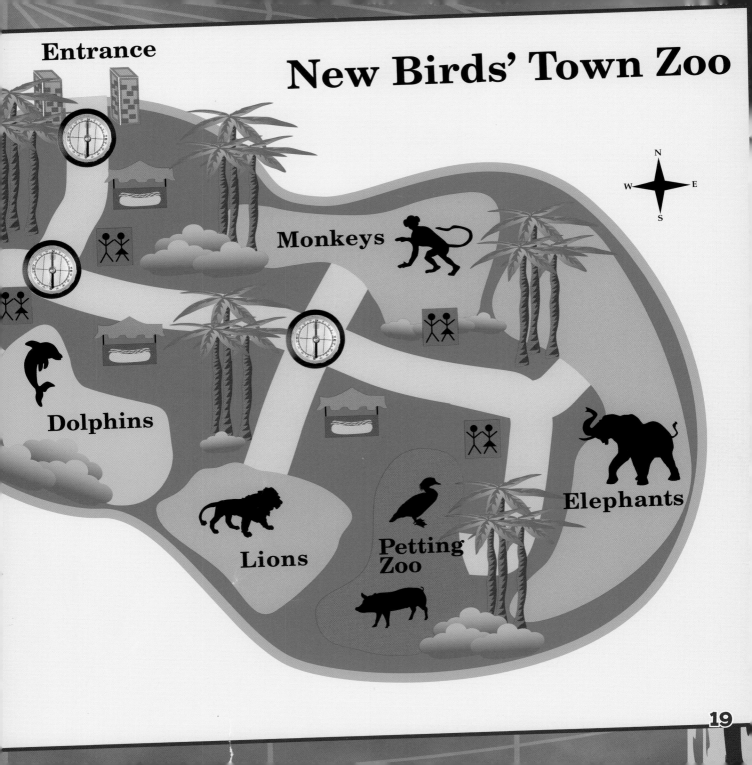

Many sea turtles swim many miles away from where they hatched. But the females return to where they hatched to lay their own eggs. How do they know how to get home? Scientists think sea turtles have a kind of compass in their brains. This compass helps them swim in the right direction.

Hands On: Make a Compass

Metal deep inside the earth creates a magnetic field around our planet. Its pull is strongest near the North Pole. That's why compass needles always point in that direction. You can make a compass that will help you find north.

What You Need

magnet
sewing needle
pin
small cork
clear plastic cup

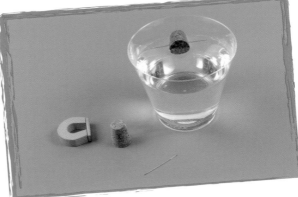

What You Do

1. Rub the magnet along the needle about 30 times in the same direction. Check to see if it is magnetized by trying to pick up a pin. If it doesn't pick up the pin, rub the needle a few more times.
2. Have an adult help you push the needle through the cork. The needle should stick out at both ends.
3. Fill the plastic cup with water. Carefully place the cork on the water. When the needle stops moving, its thickest end will be pointing north.

Glossary

compass (KUHM-puhss)—an instrument used for finding directions; a compass has a magnetic needle that always points north.

compass rose (KUHM-puhss ROZE)—a label that shows direction on a map

dial (DYE-uhl)—the face on a clock, compass, or other measuring instrument

direction (duh-REK-shuhn)—the way that someone or something is moving or pointing

Read More

Ashley, Susan. *I Can Read a Map.* I Can Do It! Milwaukee: Weekly Reader Early Learning Library, 2005.

Trumbauer, Lisa. *You Can Use a Compass.* Rookie Read-About Science. New York: Children's Press, 2003.

Internet Sites

FactHound offers a safe, fun way to find Internet sites related to this book. All of the sites on FactHound have been researched by our staff.

Here's how:
1. Visit *www.facthound.com*
2. Choose your grade level.
3. Type in this book ID **1429600551** for age-appropriate sites. You may also browse subjects by clicking on letters, or by clicking on pictures and words.
4. Click on the **Fetch It** button.

Facthound will fetch the best sites for you!

Index

compasses, 10, 12, 13, 15,
    17, 18, 20
    dials, 10, 13
    needles, 10, 12, 13
compass roses, 8

directions, 6, 8, 9, 14, 15, 17,
    18, 20

finding north, 10, 11, 13,
    17, 18

orienteering, 15

sea turtles, 20
sun, 11

using a map and
    compass, 12–13, 14–15,
        16–17, 18